Brand ★ Strategy

Workbook

Brand★Strategy
Workbook

6 Steps to Building a
Lasting Identity

Lloyd Corder, Ph.D.

CorCom, Inc.
Research & Consulting
www.corcom-inc.com

Printed in the United States of America.

Copyediting, proofreading and design by Laine Mallet and Jessica Cohen. Cover design by Sabrina Amann-Ross.

This publication is designed to provide accurate and authoritative information in regard to the subject matter covered. It is sold with the understanding that the publisher is not engaged in rendering legal, accounting or other professional services. If legal advice or other expert assistance is required, the services of a competent professional should be sought.

> -From a declaration of principles jointly adopted by a committee of the American Bar Association committee of publishers.

CorCom, Inc. books are printed on long-lasting acid-free paper. When it is available, we choose paper that has been manufactured by environmentally responsible processes. These may include using trees from sustainable forests, incorporating recycled paper, minimizing chlorine in bleaching or recycling the energy produced at the paper mill.

Contents

1
Brand

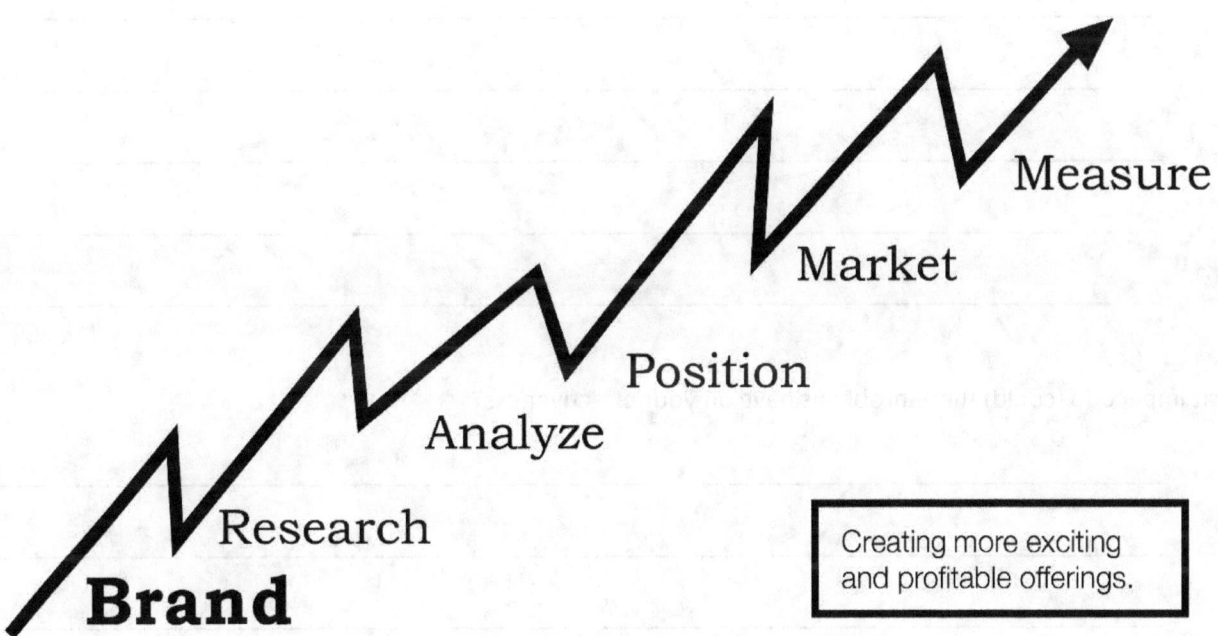

Measure

Market

Position

Analyze

Research

Brand

Creating more exciting
and profitable offerings.

List five problems or challenges that you face in trying to brand products, services, ideas—or even yourself:

1. _____

   _____

2. _____

   _____

3. _____

   _____

4. _____

   _____

5. _____

   _____

What impact do (could) these problems have on your effectiveness?

_____

_____

_____

If you could eliminate these problems, what would it mean to you professionally and personally?

_____

_____

_____

Much has been written and said about natural gas drilling in the Marcellus Shale. As a leading natural gas producer in the Appalachian basin, EQT has a unique perspective in the conversation—not only because of the business we're in, but also because of the simple fact that we live and work here in your community.

EQT is a Pittsburgh-based company, and many of our more than 1,800 employees are your neighbors, friends and family. Based on conversations with people in the communities we serve, we feel that most people understand the economic and employment potential of natural gas development. We all want good paying jobs in the hands of local people. We need to work together to develop the training and educational resources that will establish our region as a center of excellence in new natural gas development.

At the same time, we all value our land and our lifestyle, and we don't want to see that jeopardized. We have worked hard to refine and improve our production techniques so that our region and our country can benefit from these natural gas resources, which are cleaner, cheaper and much more abundant locally than imported oil, while protecting our environment. During our 120 years of operation, we have learned an important lesson: preserving the environment is good business.

EQT sets high standards when it comes to the protection of the environment and safety. EQT is committed to protecting water supplies. For instance, we conduct pre-drill testing on all domestic water sources to determine water characteristics before we ever begin drilling. EQT safeguards freshwater supplies throughout the drilling process by "triple casing" (installing multiple layers of steel casing and concrete between drilling equipment and freshwater aquifers) at each well. And, we recycle or reuse virtually all of the water produced during drilling and hydraulic fracturing.

We also understand that air quality is a serious and significant concern to Pennsylvanians. EQT continues to expand its greenhouse gas (GHG) program to quantify and reduce our total environmental footprint. Now in its third year, the program measures and assesses our GHG emissions from every source, including production wells, pipelines, compressor stations and vehicles.

Over the next few months, we intend to address such issues through community outreach to our neighbors and through a series of

informational articles on topics of importance to you. The purpose is simple: to continue our dialogue and present a range of ideas and alternatives to some of the greatest challenges facing our country, our economy and our state. We believe that ongoing dialogue with our neighbors can lead us to new ideas and solutions.

In July 2011, the Pennsylvania Marcellus Shale Advisory Commission issued a report containing 96 recommendations for our industry. This is an important first step in developing comprehensive legislation, regulation and public policy that will promote safe and responsible development of the Marcellus Shale and ensure that the communities where we have a presence have an opportunity to economically benefit from this abundant natural resource. The Commission's recommendations include enactment of an impact fee with revenues returned to localities where development is occurring, adoption of legislation and regulation to ensure environmentally responsible development, and economic development initiatives. While consensus was reached on many issues, EQT will continue to work with environmental groups to find common ground on outstanding issues. Additionally, EQT looks forward to working with the Governor, the Legislature and the Commonwealth's regulatory agencies in implementing the report's recommendations.

We're bullish on our future and committed to the communities in which we operate. Domestically produced natural gas has the ability to break America's dependence on foreign energy. It's clean. It's abundant and lies deep beneath our very feet. Our future, as a country and as a region, depends on tapping into this vast natural resource.

We are EQT. We live here. We work here. And we want to partner with you on these common goals. We look forward to continuing our discussions.

Questions

1. How are the rhetorical appeals and techniques being applied (ethos, logos, pathos) to persuade readers?

   _____

   _____

   _____

2. What impact, if any, would an ad like this have on EQT's brand?

   _____

   _____

   _____

3. Why would a natural gas company feel compelled to run such ads?

   _____

   _____

   _____

Breakout
Session

Laws of Branding

What are the "laws" of branding? Al Reis and his daughter Laura list 22 of them. Pick a product and decide which, if any, apply to the specific product as one of its core brand advantages.

The 22 Immutable Laws of Branding

In their book, *The 22 Immutable Laws of Branding*, Al and Laura Reis summarize them as following:

1. **Law of Expansion:** The power of a brand is inversely proportional to its scope. Customers want brands that are narrow in scope and are distinguishable by a word; the shorter, the better.

2. **Law of Contraction:** If you want to build a powerful brand in the minds of consumers, you need to contract your brand, not expand it. Narrow the focus. Once narrowed, dominate the category.

3. **Law of Publicity:** The birth of a brand is achieved with publicity, not advertising. Be the first brand in a new category to generate publicity. The news media wants to talk about what's new, what's first, what's hot -- not what's better. And the best way to make news is to announce a new category, not a new product.

4. **Law of Advertising:** Be a brand leader because it's the single most important motivating factor in consumer behavior. When your product/service is the leader, people think it must be better. If you tell them in your advertising that your product is better, they'll think, "That's what they all say." Advertising is a powerful tool to maintain leadership and protection from competition.

5. **Law of the Word:** If you want to build a brand, you must focus your efforts on owning a word in the prospects' mind. A word nobody else owns. Looking for ways to broaden the base, to get into other markets, capture other attributes, is one of the most common branding mistakes. You can only become generic (Kleenex, Band-Aid, Xerox) by being the first brand to establish the category. To be first in a category, create a new one by narrowing your focus. The most successful brands are those that kept a narrow focus and the expanded the category as opposed to expanding the name into other categories.

6. **Law of Credentials:** Claim authenticity. Advertising claims are perceived as puffery, unless they are structured around aspects of the brand's credentials.

7. **Law of Quality:** Quality has little to do with success in the marketplace. Quality -- or the perception of quality -- resides in the mind. A specialist (narrow focus) is perceived to know more.

8. **Law of the Category:** The leading brand should promote the category, not he brand. Increasing market share is not the most useful aspect of branding; it's creating a new category—starting something totally new.

9. **Law of the Name:** A brand is nothing more than a name. In time, the unique idea or concept of your company or product disappears. All that's left is the difference between your brand name and the brand names of your competitors.

10. **Law of Extensions:** The easiest way to destroy a brand is to put its name on everything. If the market is moving out from under you, stay where you are and launch a second brand. If it's not stay where you are and continue building your brand.

11. **Law of Fellowship:** To build a category, a brand should welcome other brands. Competition broadens the category and allows the brands to stay focused. No brand can own the entire market. Around 50% is the upper limit.

12. **Law of the Generic:** Don't give a brand a generic name.

13. **Law of the Company:** There is a difference between the brand and the company. Customers care only about brands, not companies.

14. **Law of the Sub-brands:** What branding builds, sub-branding can destroy. What "name" places an ad in the yellow pages?

15. **Law of Siblings:** There is a time and place to launch a second brand. The key to a family approach is to make each sibling a unique individual brand with its own identity -- as different and distinct as possible. The parent brand should not have to support the generic sibling. Resist the temptation to take advantage of the parent brand's equity.

16. **Law of Shape:** A logotype should be designed to fit both eyes. The real power of the brand name lies in the meaning of the word in the mind.

17. **Law of Color:** A brand should use a color that is the opposite of its major competitor's. By standardizing on a single color and using it consistently over the years, you can build a powerful visual presence in a clutter-filled world.

18. **Law of Borders:** A brand should know no borders. Keep the brand's narrow focus in its home country, and then go global. But...You need to be first. Your product needs to fit the perceptions of its country of origin.

19. **Law of Consistency:** Brand success is measured in decades, not years. A brand cannot get into the mind unless it stands for something. Once it occupies a position, it shouldn't change (bend, yes). Markets may change, but brands should stay the same. Brand building is boring. The essence of branding is limiting the brand to stand for something simple and narrow—then combine it with consistency.

20. **Law of Change:** Brands can be changed, but only infrequently and only very carefully. If you want to change your brand, first look into the prospect's mind. What's there?

21. **Law of Mortality:** No brand will live forever. Sometimes euthanasia is the best solution. A well-known brand that doesn't stand for anything (or stands for something irrelevant) has no value.

22. **Law of Singularity:** The most important aspect of a brand is its single-mindedness. A brand is a proper noun that can be used in the place of a common word. "What's a _____?" A brand is a singular idea or concept that you own inside the mind of a prospect.

Questions

Form a group and critique a product, service or other brand through the lens of Reis' 22 Laws of Branding.

Product:	

1. Which laws are they strongest in?

    _____

    _____

    _____

2. Which laws are they weakest in?

    _____

    _____

    _____

3. Is the brand's level of success established in spite of or because of the Laws of Branding?

    _____

    _____

    _____

4. Based on the brand you're critiquing, do you find that the Laws of Branding appear effective and true?

    _____

    _____

    _____

5.   Do you the find the laws to be applicable internationally?

_____

_____

_____

6.   General comments/feedback?

_____

_____

_____

Brandstorming

Brandstorming, a mix between brainstorming and branding, helps you understand your marketing situation quickly.

Storyboarding on Steroids

This technique is best when you have a group of people who have valuable perspectives and insights into your current marketing situation and possible survey question topics.

Typical Display Boards for a Brandstorming Session

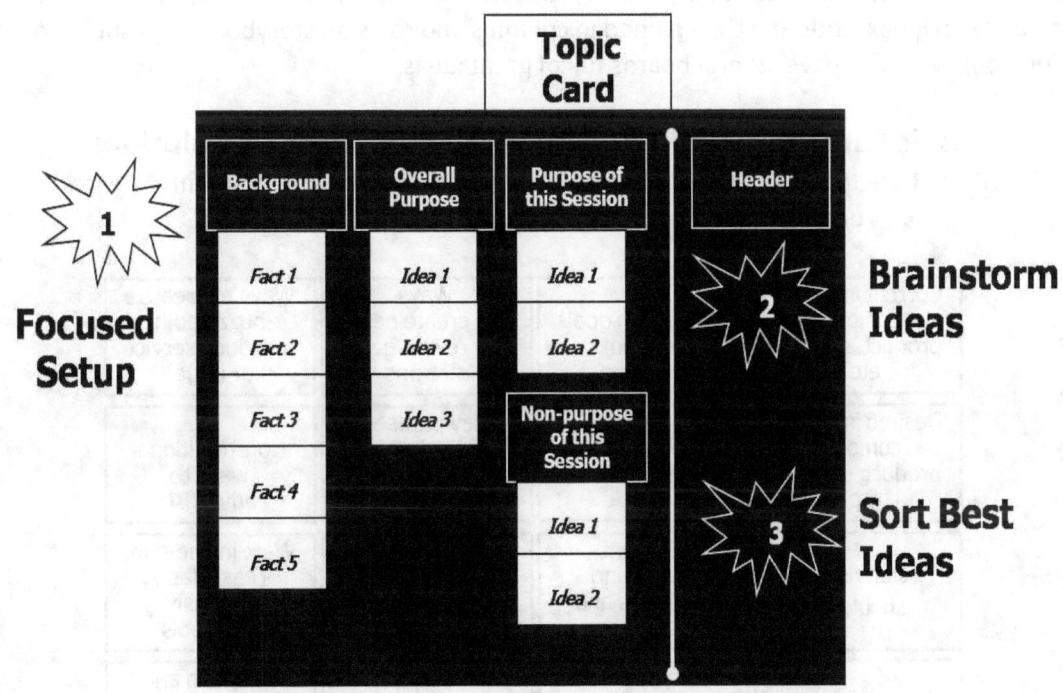

Brandstorming sessions typically follow three basic steps and can last for a few minutes to several hours or over even longer periods of time:

1. **Focused Setup:** To make sure everyone at the session is up to speed, someone should give an overview of the current situation, facts, purpose of the meeting and so on. In the chart above, the left side of the diagram shows some good categories to organize this information:

    a. Background: These are the facts such as previous research, sales information and other relevant information.

b. <u>Overall Purpose</u>: What are two or three things that you are trying to do over the next several days, weeks or months? It might be to launch a new product, solve a production problem, identify a new market, etc. Letting everyone know your broad objectives is a good way to give an overview.

c. <u>Purpose of This Session</u>: What do you want to get out of this meeting? Perhaps it is outlining a questionnaire, deciding upon a target market to ask for feedback, etc.

d. <u>Non-purpose of this Session</u>: What is out of bounds? Complaining about past issues, focusing on detailed operational issues, etc. might be meeting time wasters and should be identified before getting into the heart of the session.

2. **Brainstorm Ideas:** Next, you want to start your brainstorming session by posting "header" cards, which typically have thought-starter phrases that you want participants to focus on. The best way to solve this problem...Ways to leapfrog our competitors...Issues we are likely to encounter...and many others can help your teammates think faster and more precisely. As ideas are suggested, they are recorded accurately on index cards and then pinned in columns and rows on storyboards (pushpin boards). Before long, you may have several boards full of great ideas.

Topic Cards to Help Participants Think of Creative Solutions
(Post at the top of additional boards and pin ideas, insights or comments to each underneath them to form columns and rows of thinking.)

Current image of (company, product, service, etc.)	Short-term goals we should focus on	Ways to create new revenue streams	Ways to create a buzz about (product, service or issue)
Desired image of (company, product, service, etc.)	Long-term goals we must meet	Key phrases that will grab our target audience	Non-traditional ways to advertise
Our vision should be	Current marketing materials and approach	Cutting-edge promotional ideas we can use right away	Walk-in-the-park (easy, fast, inexpensive) ROI tools
What prospects expect and want	Ideal marketing materials and approach	Ways to become indispensable to our customers	Stunning and dramatic ways to present ROI results

3. **Sort Best Ideas:** Most sessions generate way too much information to be used in any one project, so you need to take some time to prioritize the best ideas. To do this, participants are given a limited number of brightly colored stickers and asked to place them on the ideas/cards that are most important to focus on or do. Usually, a handful of cards get the most stickers, which can then be resorted into new categories.

When the session is completed, the index cards can be taped together, pulled off the boards and used later on as an outline of ideas. In many sessions, spending 10-15 minutes on questionnaire topics is enough to generate an excellent outline, which will save you a lot of time when you start to write your survey draft.

Supplies You Will Need

To run your own Brandstorming session, you will need:

- ❑ Storyboards (or a place to post the ideas that come out).
- ❑ Flipchart stands.
- ❑ Push pins.
- ❑ Index cards (multiple sizes).
- ❑ Markers.
- ❑ Stickers (to prioritize ideas).
- ❑ Topic cards (prepared ahead of time to be posted at the top of your boards and used throughout the session).
- ❑ Transparent tape (to run down both sides of the cards that have been pinned on the board so you can later use them at your desk).

Sample Session Outline: Clamshell Community Day

Clamshell Community Day, a factious story that could be true for any beach town, is an event that is held every summer at the beach since the 1950s. As of late, the event has been dying and attendance has dropped from about 5,000 to 250. Participants are asked to participate in a brandstorming session to develop marketing strategies and tactics that can be used to turn this event around. Part of the session will involve generating ideas that can be used for measuring marketing ROI, as well as quickly creating question topics for surveys to learn visitors' perceptions about the event.

1. **Goal (What Are We Trying to Do?)**
   a. Help Make Clamshell Community Day More Successful

2. **Overall Purpose (Why Are We Here?)**
   a. Develop strategies and tactics that will improve Clamshell's Community Day attendance

3. **Purpose of This Session (What Are Today's Goals?)**
   a. Create a new strategy for promoting Community Day
   b. Develop 3-5 practical ways (tactics) to promote Community Day
   c. Establish ways to measure the success of the strategy and tactics that promote Community Day

4. **Non-purpose (What's Out of Bounds?)**
   a. Cancel the event
   b. Increase the Community Day budget more than 10 percent
   c. Lament or vent about past events
   d. Focus on operational issues

5. **Background (What Are the Facts?)**
   a. About the event:
      - Open house for the Clamshell business community
      - Generally held the weekend following the 4th of July
      - Key activities:
        o Marching bands
        o Sidewalk sales
        o Food kiosks
        o Keynote speaker
        o Late-afternoon ice cream social and tea dance

   b. Event history:
      - Launched during the Carter era
      - Originally an attempt to improve relations between townsfolk and the business community
      - Average attendance dipped from 5,000 when first started to 250 in recent years
      - Local paper covers the event but is light on ink
      - No TV or radio coverage in recent years
      - The big draw—keynote speaker

   c. Previous speakers:
      - John Wayne
      - Bill Cosby
      - Oprah
      - Pat Buchanan

   d. About the community:
      - The town has grown dramatically since the 1960s
      - Major industry is tourism
      - Population
        o 12,232 in winter
        o 20,000 in summer
        o Average age: 31
      - One daily and one weekly newspaper, one TV station and 4 radio stations in the area
      - Many young families with young children are locating in the area
      - Closest metropolitan area, River City, 50 miles to the South

   e. About the mayor:
      - Frank "Foot" Draggert
      - Father was mayor when Community Day was launched
      - Served on the initial planning committee for the event
      - At the second annual Community Day, he met his wife of 40 years, Daisy
      - While mayor is open to new ideas, still believes keynote speaker is the big draw
      - Draggert's pet notion: softball tournament will boost attendance
      - Previous marketing approach:
        o Ad placements in local newspaper two weeks prior to the event
        o Listings in community events calendars and church bulletins
        o Posters in bowling alleys, in supermarkets and downtown telephone poles

    f.   About Your staff:
- Two persons—you and an assistant

6. **Topic Headers (Session Thought-starter Cards)**
   a. Who are our prime prospects?
   b. The focus of Community Day should be...
   c. Cutting-edge advertising and promotional ideas
   d. Ways to get volunteers for Community Day
   e. Ways to get the media beating down our door
   f. Ways to get residents involved (in promoting Community Day)
   g. Easy ways to make visitors feel like VIPs
   h. Ways to get visitors excited about next year's event
   i. Easy ways to drum up visitors on the event day
   j. Ways to create a buzz about Community Day
   k. Key phrases for talking about Community Day
   l. Essential information (questions for target audiences)
   m. Easy ways to learn residents' likes/dislikes
   n. Walk in the park ROI tools (easy, fast, inexpensive)
   o. Stunning and dramatic ways to present ROI results

7. **Cards for Sorting Prioritized Results**
   a. Objectives
   b. Strategies
   c. Target Audiences
   d. Key Messages
   e. Tactics
   f. ROI

Project
Assignment

1 Agency Shootout Team Selection

- Sign-up for one of the Agency Teams

2 Team Proposal for Brand Strategy Project Team Selection

- 1-2 page write-up
- Real organization and/or product is best
- Research-based (qualitative and/or quantitative)

3 Project Brandstorming Session

- With your team, prepare a Brandstorming session outline (purpose, topic cards, etc.)
- Use sticky notes, cards on the floor other modified technique as your storyboarding tool
- Conduct the session with your team
- Summarize the key insights/findings from your session
- Turn in your session outline and summary of the session (key learnings, takeaways, etc.) and suggest any changes or improvements in terms of how the tool worked.

2

Research

Brand

Research

Analyze

Position

Market

Measure

Gathering feedback
from your target market.

Breakout
Session

Research Challenges

List five problems or challenges that you face in trying to conduct brand research:

1. _____

   _____

2. _____

   _____

3. _____

   _____

4. _____

   _____

5. _____

   _____

What impact do (could) these problems have on your effectiveness?

_____

_____

_____

If you could eliminate these problems, what would it mean to you professionally and personally?

_____

_____

_____

Sewickley Heights Golf Club Survey

Review the survey and make suggestions how to improve the questions, flow and other elements.

To all SHGC women members, spouses, and significant others,

We would like your opinions about women's golf at Sewickley Heights Golf Club (SHGC). The undersigned have received the endorsement of Joe Farrell, Chairman of the Golf Committee, and Linda Jones, President of the Sewickley Heights Women's Golf Association (SHWGA), to conduct this in depth survey.

Our goal is to identify and encourage more girls and women golfers to play our spectacular golf course and enjoy the company of friends. Please take a few minutes to fill out the enclosed survey and return it in the reply envelope by September 29th. Your comments will help guide the 2001 Women's Golf Association Board to better meet your golfing needs and interests. The results will be sent to all SHGC women and will be discussed during an open session at the Women's Golf Association end of season luncheon on October 19th. Even if you are not currently a member of the Sewickley Heights Women's Golf Association, we welcome your participation in the discussion.

Yours for better golf,

Shirley Barker   Ruth Darragh   Sue Gittins   Pat Neese   Patti Rambasek

P.S. As a thank you for your time and thoughtful consideration in filling out this survey, please enjoy two free passes to the National Aviary. There's more than one way to have birdies than on the golf course!

Sewickley Heights Women's Golf Survey

Thank you for filling out this survey. Your candid responses will further women's golf at Sewickley Heights and help us create a more viable club. We have provided extra space for you to explain your answers if you wish. Any additional comments or suggestions will be appreciated.

1. How many years have you been affiliated with SHGC?
1-2
3-5
6-10
11-15
16+

2. What is your age group?
25-35
36-45
46-55
56-65
66+

3. About how often do you play at SHGC?
1-2 rounds per year
1 round per month
2 rounds per month
4 rounds per month
1 round per week
2 rounds per week
3 + rounds per week

4. About how often do you play elsewhere during <u>our golf season</u>?
6 rounds or less per year
7-12 rounds per year
1 round per week
2 + rounds per week

5. Is there anything that prevents you from playing SHGC more than you do?
Work
Family
Volunteering
Other_____-

6. What is your interest in the game of golf?
No interest
Some interest
Moderate interest

High interest

7. If you have some or moderate interest in golf, what would increase your involvement in the game?

8. We believe teenage girls, especially, lose interest in golf - never to return or return only years later. Do you have a suggestion how we can encourage SHGC teen girls to continue with the sport?

Non-SHWGA Members
(SHWGA members, please skip to the next section.)

9. Have you ever been a member of the SHWGA?
Yes   No

10. Why did you let your membership lapse?

11. What would it take for you to join the association?

12. Would you be interested in joining a 9 hole league?
Yes No

13. Would you like to participate in a golf clinic?
   Yes No

14. Would you join the SHWGA if there were less competition and more open play?
   Yes No

15. Would you join the SHWGA if you were given a SHWGA mentor the first year?
Yes No

Sewickley Heights Women's Golf Association Members

16. How long have you been a member?
1-2 years
3-5 years
5-10 years
11- 15 years
16 + years

17. What was your reason for joining?

18. Why do you continue your membership?

19. How often do you play in the SHWGA Thursday events?
Guest days only
Once per month
Twice per month
Three times per month

20. What would increase your participation in the SHWGA?

21. What do you like best about the SHWGA?

22. What do you like least about the SHWGA?

23. Which do you prefer for Thursday golf?
    More competitive golf
    Less competitive golf

24. Would you prefer to have one or more Thursdays "open play" as the men have on
    Saturdays?
Keep the Thursday play the same
Open play once per month
Open play twice per month

25. Do you like the way the regular Thursday play is organized? Please be specific.

26. Do you have any suggestion for the tournament events listed in your association
    yearbook? Please be specific.

27. How friendly do you feel the SHWGA is to newcomers?
Not friendly
Moderately friendly
Very friendly

28. How friendly do you feel SHWGA is to regular members?
Not friendly
Moderately friendly
Very freindly

29. Do you feel the Board keeps you well-informed?
Yes. No.

29. Instead of an opening luncheon and a closing luncheon, what would you prefer?
 Breakfast meeting
 Dinner meeting

30. What day would you prefer the meetings to be?

Tuesday, Wednesday, Thursday, Friday, Saturday, Sunday

31. Would you be interested in becoming more involved in the governance and planning of the SHWGA?

Yes No

(If yes, please make your interest known to the SHWGA Board so you can become involved in planning for the 2001 golf season. We welcome your ideas and your time!)

What other comments and suggestions can you make about the golf environment for women and girls at SHGC?

Your name (optional)_____

Thank you for your participation in this survey!

Project
Assignment

1. Agency Shootout #1: Teams 1, 2 & 3

- Everyone else, be ready to ask questions, provide recommendations, etc. to the presenters
- Representatives from the client will be here as well

2. Brand Assessment Research Tool (Survey, Moderator's Guide or Others)

- Design your brand assessment tool and research approach
- Bring 5-10 printed copies of it to class for a "scratch and pass" exercise (start of next session). Following that, make any changes or improvements and turn in.

3
Analyze

Measure

Market

Position

Analyze

Research

Brand

Working with your data to discover valuable insights.

After circulating 5-10 printouts of your questionnaire, online form, moderator's guide or other research tool, what insights did you gain about your current draft? What could be modified to further improve it?

1. _____

_____

2. _____

_____

3. _____

_____

4. _____

_____

5. _____

_____

From reviewing others' instruments, what techniques or approaches seemed to work <u>best</u>?

1. _____

_____

2. _____

_____

3. _____

_____

From reviewing others' instruments, what <u>common problems or issues</u> did you find?

1. _____

   _____

2. _____

   _____

3. _____

   _____

Analysis Challenges

List five problems or challenges that you face in trying to analyze data:

1. _____

_____

2. _____

_____

3. _____

_____

4. _____

_____

5. _____

_____

What impact do (could) these problems have on your effectiveness?

_____

_____

_____

If you could eliminate these problems, what would it mean to you professionally and personally?

_____

_____

_____

Cleaning Data in Excel

Getting your data file "clean" and ready to analyze is one of the most important steps in the research process.

The first step in data analysis is to clean your data (making sure that everyone who should have answered a question did, and making sure those who should not have answered, did not). Also, it might make sense to code your open-ended questions into categories so you can summarize them and compare them to other answers.

The goal is to get your data into columns (variables) and rows (individual responses) that make sense and are accurate with skip to's, etc.

1. If not already in Excel, select the data that you plan to clean from your online data collection or other tool and insert it into a blank worksheet.

2. Paste it in cell B3 if the top row of your file includes the names of your variables (e.g., actual question or Q1, Q2, etc.). If not, paste data in cell B4 and put variable names starting in B3 moving toward the right.

    > Tip: Highlight the data from the file you are bringing it in from (*Ctrl+C to copy*) and click in cell. Paste it as **values** (without formatting) by clicking the dropdown box under the paste icon in top left and choosing the option on the left

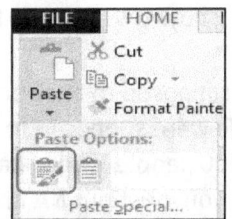

3. In cell A3, insert a variable name called "ID" for your survey Identification Number. Then, in cell A4-A6, insert a 1, 2, 3, highlight those cells and drag numbers down until all survey responses have an ID. This step will save lots of heartache if you need to restore your data back to its original organization.

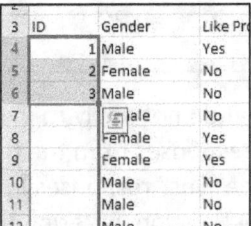

4. Highlight all of your data (including the variable names) and click Insert Table or use "**CTRL+T**" shortcut. This will put filters at the top of your table and any pivot tables or other calculations you later build can be easily created from here.

Insert table

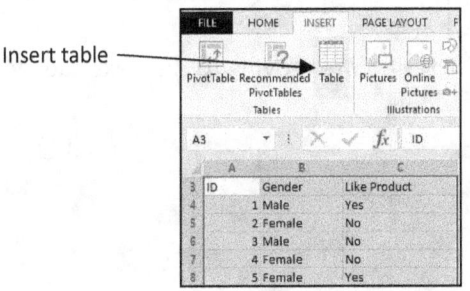

Filters:
Click down arrow to view options

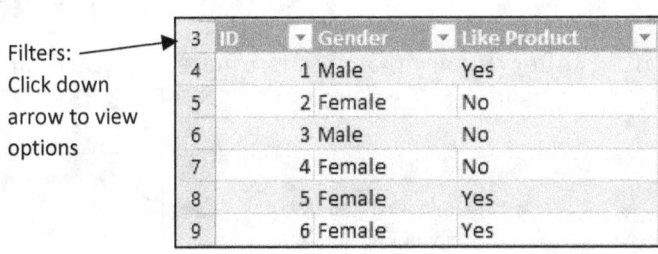

5. Some of your data may look like numbers but actually be text. Highlight the cells in question and click the icon near the first cell then choose convert to numbers.

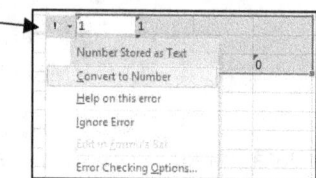

6. In cell A1, add a count formula to the top of your data. Type in the formula box =COUNT and highlight the data in column A below you want to count starting in cell A3 and going downward. Use =COUNTA for columns that are filled with text. Make sure you leave a row between counts and variables.

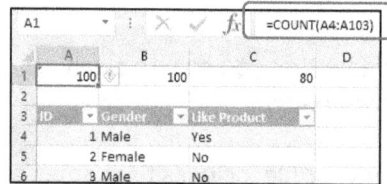

7. Drag the cell with the count formula in it across the row for all of your variables (remember =COUNTA for text). This will now tell you how many people have answered each question, also known as the base.

8. If everyone was supposed to answer a question, then your base should be the total for the survey. If only some people were supposed to answer then it will be less. Correct any bases that are incorrect. For example, if 100 people is your base, and for a question that everyone should have answered, the count is only 80, you must put NA in the 20 blank cells to make your statistics accurate. Using filters to display only the blank cells will make this a quick fix.

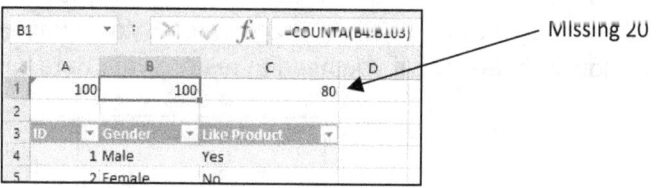

9. How to do a skip-to: For questions that do not apply to everyone, use filters to select the data in question. For example, if only "yes" responses from the previous question were supposed to answer the follow-up question, then select the "yes" responses in the filter. Make sure there is an answer for the follow-up questions for every "yes" person, entering NA for any blanks. Then, select the "no" responses and make sure all of the cells in the follow-up question column are blank. This way, only the people who were supposed to answer actually will have data in your file.

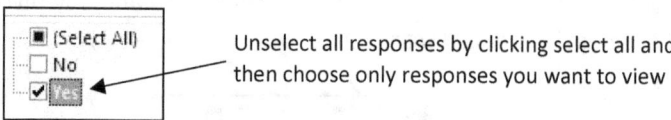

Unselect all responses by clicking select all and then choose only responses you want to view

10. After cleaning that question, make sure you clear your filter before moving to the next question and repeating the process.

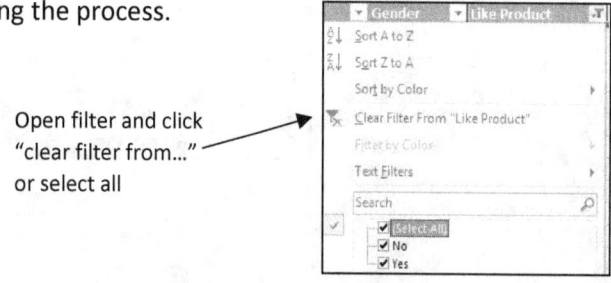

Open filter and click "clear filter from…" or select all

36

11. For open-ended questions you should plan to code them into groups. Insert a column to the right of the one that includes the open-ended comments. Read through a number of the comments and develop 1-10 categories that describe the themes. Line-by-line, go through your survey form and put numbers in the cells of your new column for each response.

If someone left an answer blank, enter NA for the response.

If a lot of people are making multiple comments, add multiple rows and use the same codes but insert them into additional columns.

If everyone is making a few (3-5) similar comments, consider entering 5+ new columns for each of the comments, then enter a "yes/no" in every cell. Recoding your open-ended questions will allow you to summarize the frequency of comments and compare them with all of your other questions.

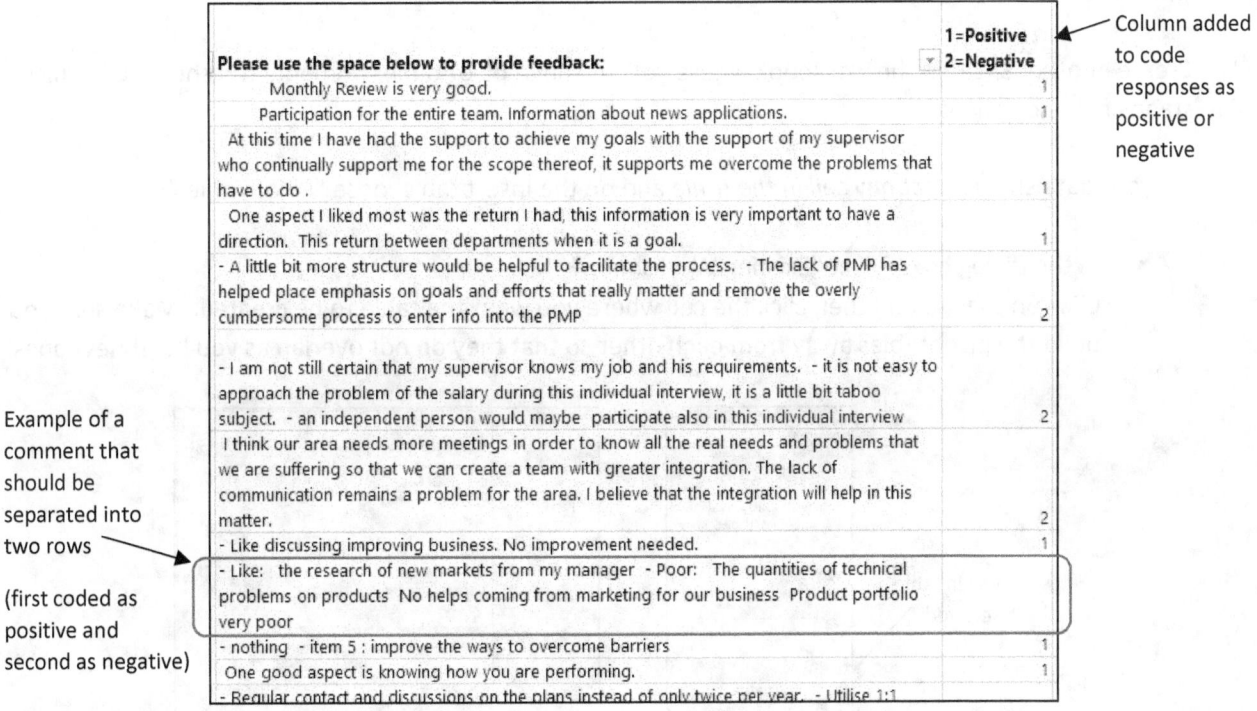

In addition to using formulas to build Excel dashboards, you can also use Pivot Tables, Slicers and graphs to get all of your data to change when selecting different groups or subsets of your responses.

The goal is to get Excel to interactively present your data and allow for easy updates...in a relatively small file size that can be easily emailed.

Pivot Tables

1. Start by inserting a table for your data file. Highlight your data and click "**CTRL+T**" (Tables allow for easy update of reports whenever data is added. Also, pivot tables can only be created from a table). Rename the sheet "D" for data by double clicking on the tab at the bottom.

2. Create another sheet in the workbook where you will build pivot tables. Rename the sheet "C", which stands for calculations.

3. On your data sheet *select any cell in the table* and on the Insert tab choose "Pivot Table."

    -   In the dialog box, select "Existing Worksheet."
    -   Click on *sheet C* and then click the cell where you want the table to be created. Make sure you build the pivot tables away from each other so that they do not overlap as you build new ones.

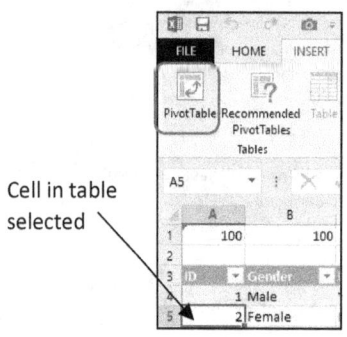
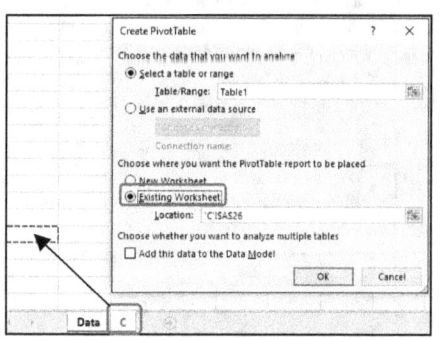

4. In PivotTable Fields on the right, check off the box next to the variable you want the table to represent and then drag it into the Row **and** Values boxes.

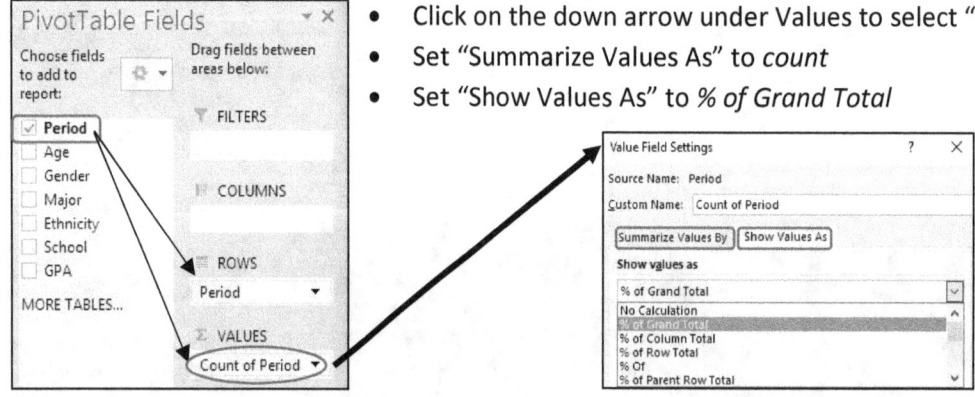

    -   Click on the down arrow under Values to select "Value Field Settings."
    -   Set "Summarize Values As" to *count*
    -   Set "Show Values As" to *% of Grand Total*

5. Use decimal rounding button to make percentages whole numbers (this cleans up your report).

Pivot Table should look like this:

Row Labels	Count of Period
2014	25.00%
2015	50.00%
2016	25.00%
Grand Total	100.00%

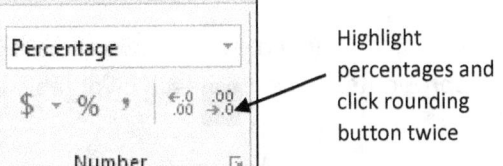

Highlight percentages and click rounding button twice

6. Click Analyze tab and change the name of the Pivot table to shorthand name of the variable/question.

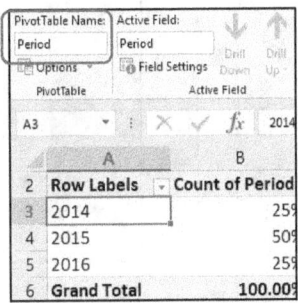

Slicers

7. Put your curser in the pivot table. On Insert tab, choose Slicer and then pick the corresponding variable. This will make a slicer for that pivot table. Repeat this for all of your pivot tables.

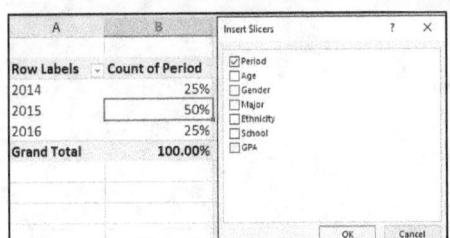
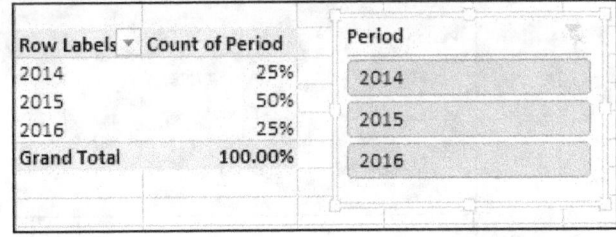

8. Click on slicer and in the top left of the Slicer Tools tab, name slicer to match Pivot Table.

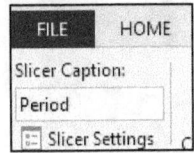

9. Under Slicer Tools select "Report Connections" and check off all the boxes. This collects all of the slicers. So, when you change data in one, all of your data changes.

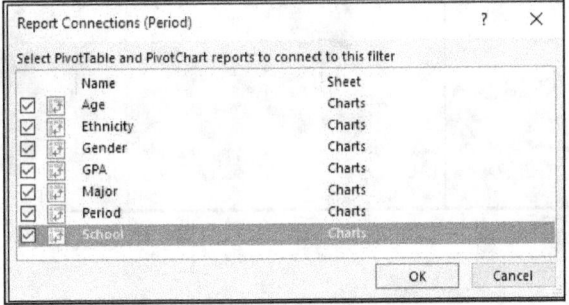

Graphs

10.   Put your curser in the pivot table and click Insert, graph. Make a pie chart or bar graph or whatever is appropriate. Repeat for each pivot table or graph that you want.

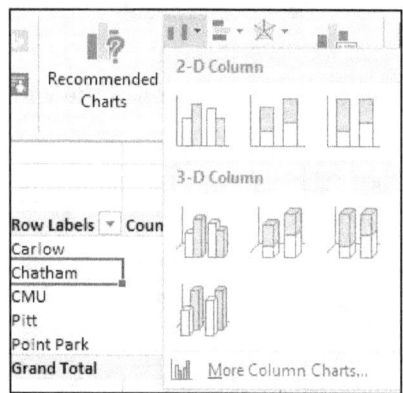 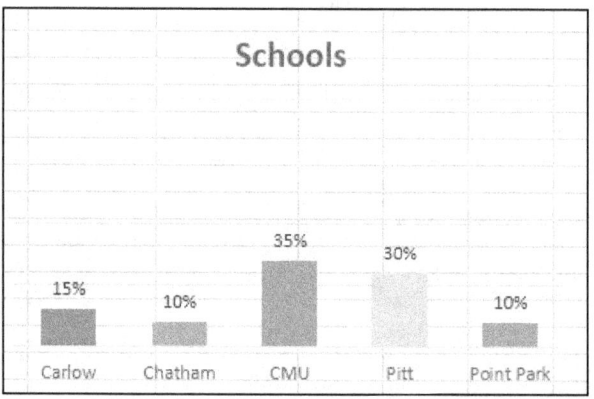

Modify the design of your charts as you like and put copies of your slicers and graphs on a separate sheet, laid out in a logical, attractive manner. If working properly, when you change the data in once slicer, all of your charts should also change.

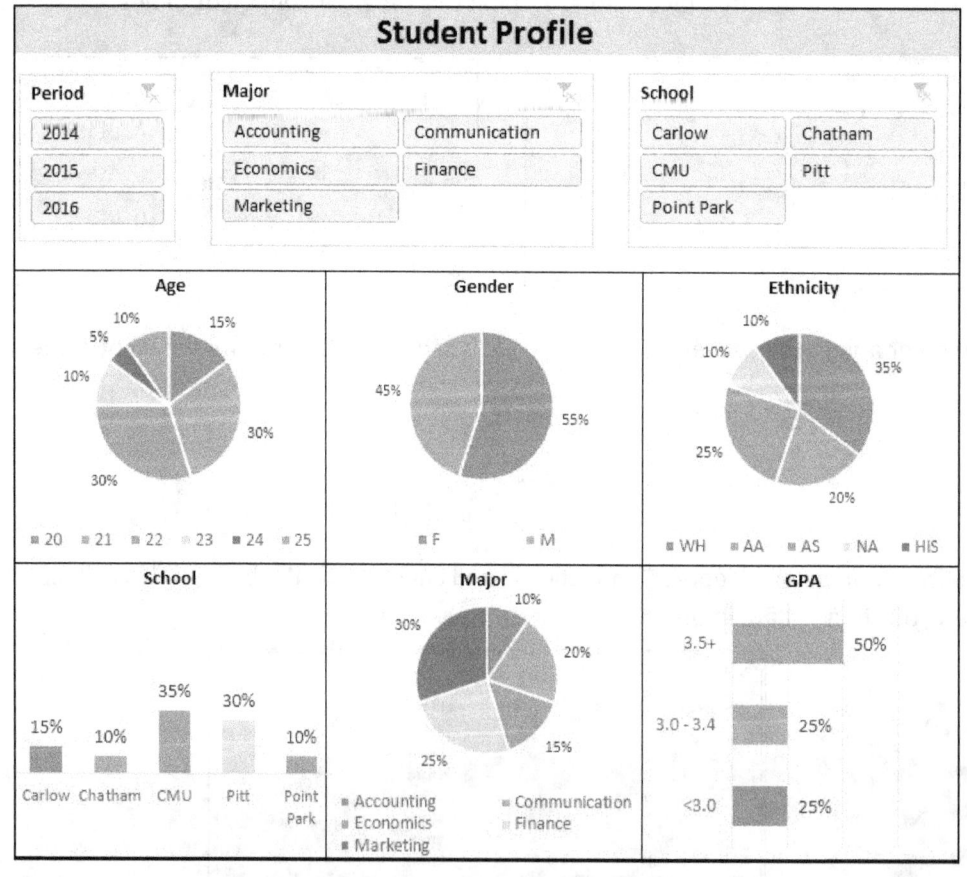

 **Project**
Assignment

1. **Agency Shootout #2: Teams 4, 5, & 6**

   - Everyone else, be ready to ask questions, provide recommendations, etc. to the presenters

2. **Brand Assessment Project**

   - Start collecting your brand data, analyzing it, etc.

4
Position

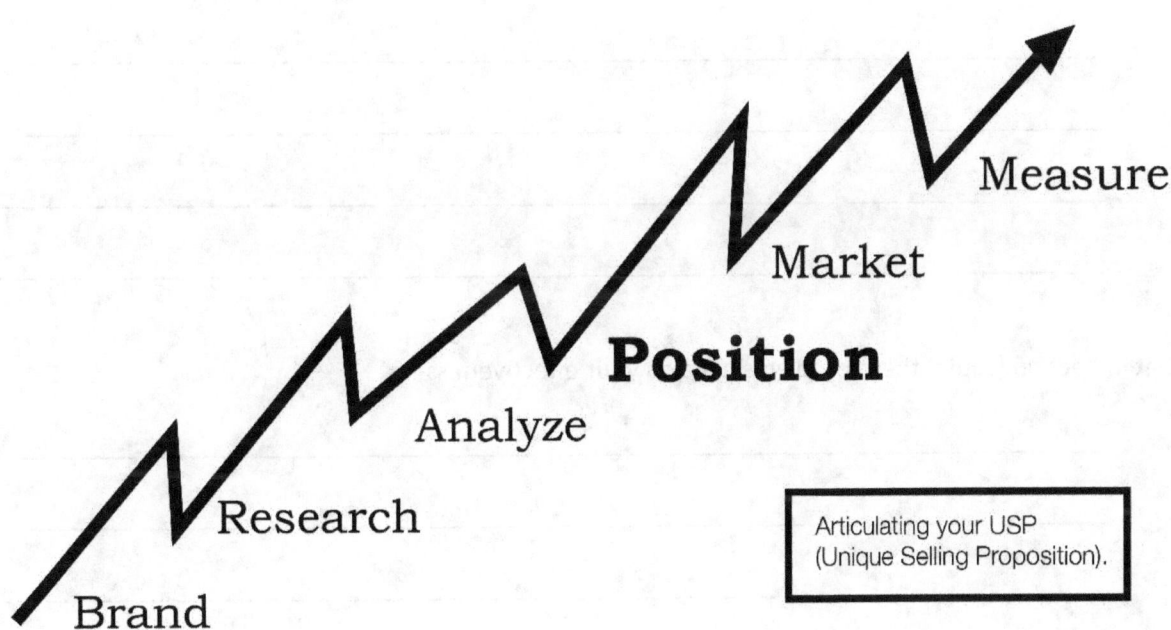

Brand

Research

Analyze

Position

Market

Measure

Articulating your USP
(Unique Selling Proposition).

Breakout
Session

Positioning Challenges

List five problems or challenges that you face (or think you will face) in trying to position your products, services or ideas:

1. _____

   _____

2. _____

   _____

3. _____

   _____

4. _____

   _____

5. _____

   _____

What impact do (could) these problems have on your effectiveness?

_____

_____

_____

If you could eliminate these problems, what would it mean to you professionally and personally?

_____

_____

_____

Brand Resonance Pyramid

Kevin Lane Keller, author of *Strategic Brand Management*, suggests using his pyramid and related questions to better understand your brand's value to customers. Apply his model to two different types of products.

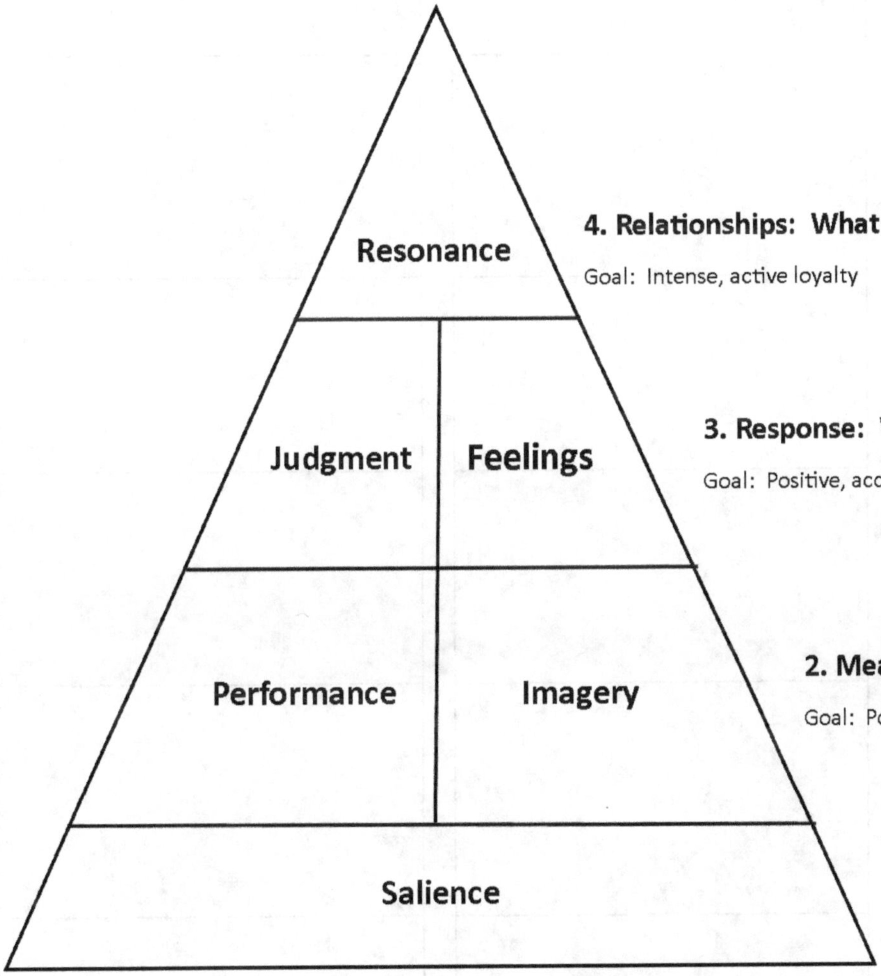

Resonance

Judgment   **Feelings**

Performance   **Imagery**

Salience

4. Relationships: What about you and me?

Goal: Intense, active loyalty

3. Response: What about you?

Goal: Positive, accessible reactions

2. Meaning: What are you?

Goal: Points-of-parity and -difference

1. Identity: Who are you?

Goal: Deep, broad brand awareness

	Product 1:	Product 2:
Salience • Brand fit in category? • How often thought about?		
Performance • How well provides: • Basic functions/needs? • Special features? • Reliability, durable, stylish, price?		
Imagery • Admired? • Like people who use the brand? • Availability?		
Judgments • Quality? • Credibility? • Willing to recommend? • Superiority?		
Feelings • Warmth? • Fun? • Excitement? • Social approval? • Self-respect?		
Resonance • Buy this brand whenever I can? • Love brand, special? • Talk about this brand?		

Developing a Concept Statement, Tagline & Elevator Presentation

Concept statements are not about you. They are about positioning what you offer in terms of the outcome of what your product, service or idea does for customers.

Concept Statement

Try creating your own positioning statement by transforming your title, products and services into a statement that your prospects will find attractive and motivating. Do not give up too quickly. It has taken many people six months or longer to think out and refine their statements before they find something with which they are completely comfortable.

1.   **Title:** What nouns do people use to describe what you do or your overall classification?

_____

_____

_____

2.   **Products/Services:** What do you offer to customers and prospects?

_____

_____

_____

3.   **Concept:** What primary benefits do customers receive from working with you?

_____

_____

_____

Tagline

Based on the value you (or your product or service) delivers to customers, what possible words could you use in a brief tagline?

_____   _____   _____

_____   _____   _____

_____   _____   _____

_____   _____   _____

_____   _____   _____

_____   _____   _____

_____   _____   _____

_____   _____   _____

_____   _____   _____

_____   _____   _____

What are the top 3 words you could use as your tagline?

_____   _____   _____

Elevator Presentation

If building an elevator presentation about yourself, a simple next step is to think of three or four "professional" bullets (products and/or services, etc.) and three or four "personal" bullets. Professional bullets are the key messages or ideas you are trying to get across. They are the big idea you want people to understand about what you do. Professional bullets focus more on the roles you play and how you can make a difference for clients.

Professional Bullets

Questions to Help You Create "Professional" Bullets:

- What do you do and how long have you been doing it?

  _____

  _____

- What markets do you serve?

  _____

  _____

- How do your customers benefit most by working with you (or using your products / services)?

  _____

  _____

For an example on writing "professional" bullets I will share mine. One of the "professional" bullets that work for me is:

- "I am a business school professor working in the real world." I go on to explain that the same things business school professors do—research, teach, consult is also what I do (marketing research, executive seminars, marketing/sales/communications counseling).

Personal Bullets

Questions to Help You Create "Personal" Bullets:

- What do you like to do for fun?

  _____

  _____

- What would we find you doing on your day off?

  _____

  _____

- What is something interesting or unique about yourself that other people might not know?

  _____

  _____

For an example on writing "personal" bullets I will share another. On the "personal" side, this line has gotten me a lot of laughs over the years:

- "A few years ago, my wife and I won the lottery. Is not that great? But it was not the Pennsylvania, Ohio or West Virginia lottery—it was the twin daughter lottery. And a few years after that, we won the single kid lottery. I am proud to tell you that I have accomplished one of my life's goals—I am surrounded by women."

Pleasure/Pain Positioning

Pleasure (feels good, attraction) and pain (want to reduce, eliminate) are both powerful motivators in terms of positioning a product or service. For each type of product or service, do you believe they are better positioned as a pleasure or pain? Why?

Product/Service	Type of Purchase Is More of...		Why?
	Pleasure	Pain	
Personal vehicle			
Tires			
Tax preparation			
Ice cream cone			
Sporting event ticket			
Funeral arrangements			

Pick a specific product or service, then develop five potential pain questions you could ask to uncover someone's pains.

Product/Service:

1. _____

_____

2. _____

_____

3. _____

_____

4. _____

_____

5. _____

_____

Project
Assignment

1. **Agency Shootout #3: Teams 7, 8, & 9**

   - Everyone else, be ready to ask questions, provide recommendations, etc. to the presenters

5
Market

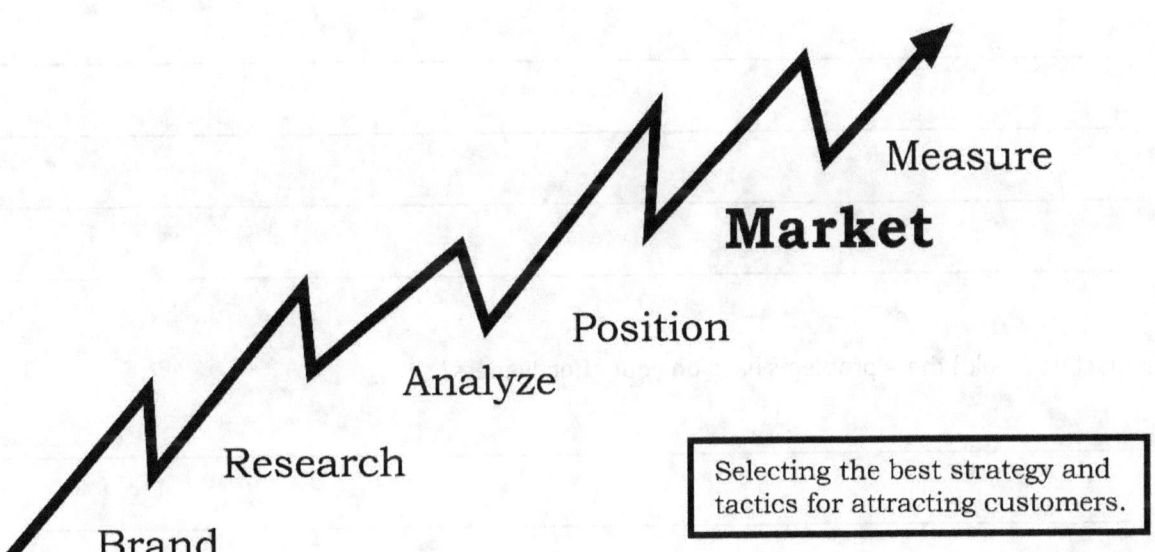

Brand

Research

Analyze

Position

Market

Measure

Selecting the best strategy and
tactics for attracting customers.

Marketing Challenges

List five problems or challenges that you face (or think you will face) in trying to market your products, services or ideas:

1. _____

   _____

2. _____

   _____

3. _____

   _____

4. _____

   _____

5. _____

   _____

What impact do (could) these problems have on your effectiveness?

_____

_____

_____

If you could eliminate these problems, what would it mean to you professionally and personally?

_____

_____

_____

Marketing Mix

Pick a product or service for each of the types of organizations below. Then, suggest how you might structure your marketing mix, key messages and other elements to best reach and persuade your

Form a group and critique a product, service or other brand for consumers, B2B and professional services. Then suggest key tactics and messages.

Consumer Product/Service:	

1. What tactics would be included in a marketing plan?

_____

_____

_____

_____

_____

_____

2. What messages should be communicated?

_____

_____

_____

3. What could be done to ensure an integrated campaign?

_____

_____

_____

B2B Product/Service:	

1.   What tactics would be included in a marketing plan?

_____

_____

_____

_____

_____

_____

2.   What messages should be communicated?

_____

_____

_____

3.   What could be done to ensure an integrated campaign?

_____

_____

_____

Professional Services Product/Service:	

1.   What tactics would be included in a marketing plan?

_____

_____

_____

_____

_____

_____

2.   What messages should be communicated?

_____

_____

_____

3.   What could be done to ensure an integrated campaign?

_____

_____

_____

Project
Assignment

1. Prepare a Draft of a Dashboard for Your Brand Strategy Project

- Based on the data you have collected so far, design an interactive dashboard to help communicate the findings of your research.

- Consider the layout, style, key conclusions, etc. that you want to communicate in your reporting.

6

Measure

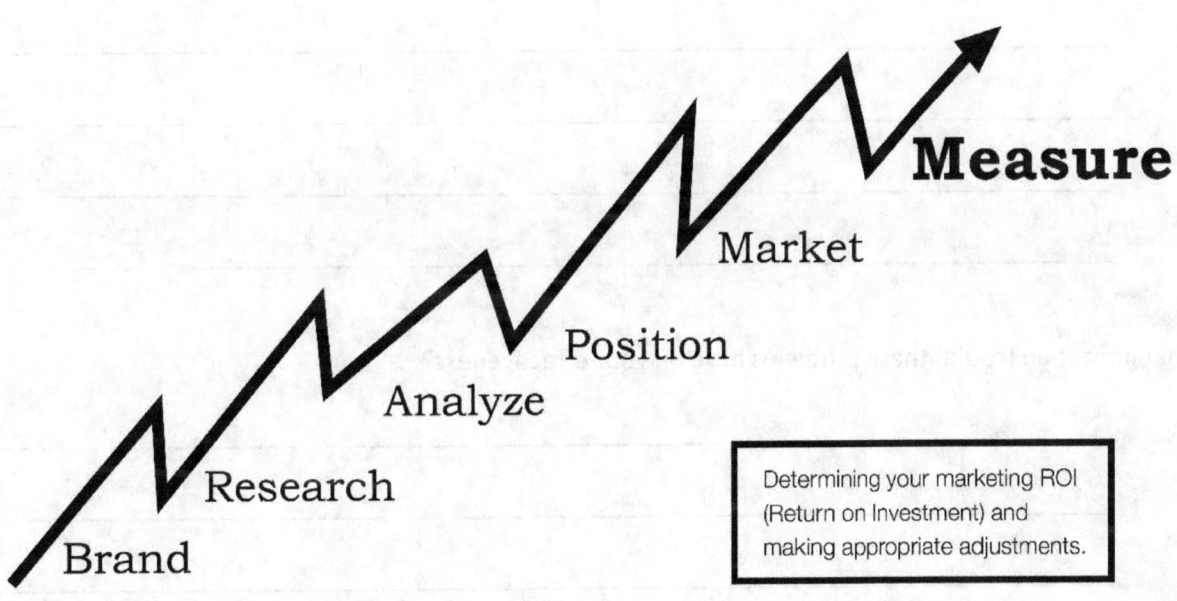

Brand

Research

Analyze

Position

Market

Measure

Determining your marketing ROI
(Return on Investment) and
making appropriate adjustments.

Marketing ROI Challenges

List five problems or challenges that you face (or think you will face) in trying to measure your market ROI:

1. _____

_____

2. _____

_____

3. _____

_____

4. _____

_____

5. _____

_____

What impact do (could) these problems have on your effectiveness?

_____

_____

_____

If you could eliminate these problems, what would it mean to you professionally and personally?

_____

_____

_____

Assessing the Value of Media Coverage

Your team is to evaluate the media coverage received for a recent public awareness campaign designed to increase consumer awareness of the telephone number 7-1-1.

As 9-1-1 is for emergencies and 4-1-1 is for information, 7-1-1 allows a deaf or hard of hearing person to communicate with a hearing person through a translator (operator). Also called relay, TRS, TT, TTD, TTD, VCO phone and CapTel phone, the system works by having both parties communicate through a telephone company employee who speaks exactly what the deaf or hard of hearing individual says to the hearing person and translates (through sign language on a video screen, Internet and other devices) what the hearing person says back to the deaf or hard of hearing individual.

While a very important resource for individuals who are deaf or hard of hearing, the 7-1-1 number and related technology is not widely known or understood by the hearing community. As a result, a lot of people simply hang up when they get one of these calls and cause continuing frustration for the system users. Therefore, the marketing campaign designed to increase awareness was launched that included radio, newspaper, bus and billboard ads, elementary school educational programs and a media relations (public relations) components—all designed to help educate the hearing community.

Summary of Media Coverage

Publication	Length of Article (Column Inches)	Circulation	Advertising Rate (Per Inch)
ABC Paper	14.50	178,241	$129.05
Small Town Gazette	10.25	81,221	$103.75
Rural News	6.00	15,567	$75.58
The Weekender	7.00	6,571	$47.95
News Online	15.00	22,058	$16.75
Inquirer	15.75	1,472,813	$160.37
Tribune	10.75	92,672	119.48
Times-Leader	6.50	22,501	75.94

<u>Media Story from ABC Paper</u>

You might know about 9-1-1 and 4-1-1, but unless you or a loved one has a hearing or speech impairment, you probably never thought about dialing 7-1-1. If you did, it would put you in touch with a communications assistant who helps deaf, hard of hearing or speech-disabled people talk on the phone.

Yesterday, a campaign to raise awareness of the phone service through billboards, radio and print ads, school programs and other activities was launched.

According to a spokesman John Smith, a campaign goal is to educate the hearing public so that people don't hang up on relay calls, which typically begin with a delay and a beep. "If you're a business, a doctor's office or restaurant, you may be hanging up on a customer," he said. "Someone who is deaf, hard of hearing or speech disabled may be calling you."

About one in 17 people have hearing or speech loss, and the problem could grow as the population ages.

A statewide survey that was completed in November 2003 revealed that 98 percent of participants knew that 9-1-1 was an emergency number and that 79 percent knew that 4-1-1 provides information on telephone numbers. But of the hearing public, "only 9 percent know about 7-1-1," Smith said.

Questions

How many impressions did this campaign receive?

_____

_____

_____

What is the ad dollar value/advertising equivalency of this campaign?

_____

_____

_____

What is the CPM for each media outlet?

_____

_____

_____

Based on the ABC Paper article, what elements would you include in a content analysis form to evaluate this and other stories?

_____

_____

_____

What additional measures, if any, do you think should be considered to evaluate this campaign?

_____

_____

_____

How successful was this campaign and why?

_____

_____

_____

Breakout
Session

Your team is to evaluate the media coverage received for a recent public awareness campaign designed to increase consumer awareness of the telephone number 7-1-1.

List three of your goals as you would normally write them or tell them to others.

1. _____

   _____

   _____

2. _____

   _____

   _____

3. _____

   _____

   _____

Goal Critique

Rewrite your goals from the previous page by making them SMART (Specific, Measurable, Attainable, Realistic and Time-Bounded). Focus on how they might solve a customers' paid or be even more valuable than first worded.

1. _____

    _____

    _____

2. _____

    _____

    _____

3. _____

    _____

    _____

Action Plans

Once you have a clearly written goal, it is important to identify all of the major steps it will take to accomplish each goal—especially if it includes doing something that you have never done before. Without an action plan, it is difficult to manage your goals, accomplish them as planned or know how much time, energy, money and other resources will be needed to reach them.

For one of the goals you have rewritten, create a detailed action plan:

Step	Activity	Deadline

MROI Plan for a Local Diner

A local diner has a basic marketing campaign that includes online media, directory advertising, sponsoring local community organizations and more. How should it measure its marketing ROI?

What program measures (overall success) would you recommend?

_____

_____

_____

_____

_____

_____

_____

What tactical measures would you recommend?

_____

_____

_____

_____

_____

_____

_____

How should they go about building their ROI tools (collecting, reporting data, managing the process)?

_____

_____

_____

_____

_____

_____

_____

_____

Project
Assignment

1. Prepare Your Brand Strategy Project Final Presentation

- Your team should deliver a 10-15 minute summary of your key conclusions and insights from your project.

- Finalize your interactive dashboard and turn it in as part of your final project deliverables.

About the Author

Lloyd Corder, Ph.D., is founder and CEO of strategic marketing research firm CorCom, Inc. and teaches at Tepper School of Business at Carnegie Mellon University and the University of Pittsburgh. He is a frequent keynote, convention and motivational speaker, and he has appeared on business-oriented radio and television programs. Corder's studies have been published in more than 500 magazines and newspapers.

Recent books, free resources and other helpful materials are available at CorCom, Inc.'s website or directly from the company. You can also order this and other printed books or Kindle downloads from Amazon (www.amazon.com).

CorCom, Inc.
www.corcom-inc.com
info@corcom-inc.com
412.201.2636